701

The Cairo

of Naguib Mahfouz

The *Cairo*
of Naguib Mahfouz

Photographs by **Britta Le Va**
Text by **Gamal al-Ghitani**
Foreword by **Naguib Mahfouz**

The American University in Cairo Press

Contents

Foreword

NAGUIB MAHFOUZ

MY LOVE AND ATTACHMENT TO OLD CAIRO are unequaled. There are many times when I feel desiccated—experiencing one of those occasional blocks to which writers are prone. Then I take a stroll through old Cairo, and almost immediately I am besieged by a host of images. It

is in old Cairo that I have imagined most of my novels. It is there that they have taken place, in my mind before I commit them to paper. And whenever I have felt that an event or an episode in my writing needs to be anchored in a specific place, al-Gamaliya has been that place. What has given me the greatest pleasure is the wonderful way in which Britta Le Va's photographs reflect the real life of today, as they remind me of the past beauty of the well-civilized centuries.

Britta Le Va has managed through her book to stir in me a longing for the beautiful place and the bygone days, for the old Cairo whose air I first breathed when I was ushered into the world, on December 11, 1911; since that time al-Gamaliya has become a center, a refuge, and an abode, with its conglomeration of cafés, squares, roads, lanes, and alleys and its ancient mosques and minarets. Wherever one directs one's eyes one beholds a minaret, an awesome, decorated entrance, a beautifully written passage from the Qur'an; or one will hear a hymn of an unknown dervish who chanted words of wisdom, or tried to reveal some kind of mystery, then was gone. Those were the inhabitants of the city, with their traits and heritage, their joys and sorrows, and their daily endeavors in the course of time. They come from all walks of life: traders, workers, artisans, makers of amulets, hawkers, civil servants, café clients, toughs, and dervishes who seek refuge behind the high walls of their *takiya*s (monasteries).

All those characters are constantly racing in my memory and in my soul, the shadows of the place, the voices of those gone, and the clamor of the passersby. Each one has a place in time and space, each one has a point of departure for which he longs and adopts as a refuge, to go back to in times of difficulties or when he is away from it. My place is in old Cairo, in al-Gamaliya to be exact. My soul is there always in spite of the passing of long years.

I have known Britta for some years now and have perceived her bursting vigor and her love for Cairo, the city of all cities. My friends spoke to me about her knowledge of the place and her discovery of the area's points of beauty. When I went in her company to the Sihaymi House she was moving with such familiarity and assurance that one would think she were the daughter of the district, born and brought up there. One

is often associated with a certain place in this world, not necessarily where one was born or where one lived. This is apparent in Britta's love for Cairo with all its different ages—the pharaonic, the Coptic, the Islamic— and through her penetrating eye she has recorded the areas of art and beauty and the radiance of creativity. She saw what could not be seen in the middle of the throng of everyday life; through a sensitive eye she has displayed samples of the artistic works with which Cairo overflows. In this book she presents the imposing buildings in meticulous details and with a uniqueness of vision. This is the result of her years of association with Cairo, of a journey that is unique and beautiful, a journey in time whose core is humanity and whose point of departure is old Cairo, where there is a constant longing for the beautiful times. This is truly a book of fond memories.

Discovering Cairo through Naguib Mahfouz

BRITTA LE VA

WHEN I WAS A YOUNG CHILD my father read the tales of the *Arabian Nights* to me. That distant past came into sharp focus as I entered Cairo's historic Fatimid city, al-Qahira, for the first time in 1989. Some people say that a storyteller who lived in Cairo in the fifteenth century collected the tales and that the locations reflect Cairo more then Baghdad.

These stories of fantasy, sensuality, melancholy, and terror left a deep impression on my young mind. So much so that I was for ever searching for the romantic visions of the Orient. French romantic writers, Orientalist painters, and the accounts of travelers lengthened the chain of connection.

Finally in 1989 I entered Cairo through the old gate of Bab al-Futuh, unknowingly walking down the processional street of the Fatimids, called al-Mu'izz li-Din Allah, which becomes Bayn al-Qasrayn (Palace Walk),

the title of the first volume of Naguib Mahfouz's *Cairo Trilogy*. As so many before me, confronted with a history dating back to at least the second century B.C., I surrendered to the irresistible malady of falling under the spell of Cairo, indeed of Egypt as a whole.

Walking through the ancient streets, contemplating the then nameless mosques and minarets, the hidden lives, the sound of the Arabic language that turned everything into poetry, the overpowering scent of dust and spices mixed with perfume, and the life of Cairo where magic and mystery beckon from every doorway—all this made me feel that I had come upon a long-forgotten dream. I felt the burning desire to conquer and possess this amazing city.

The first chapter of Naguib Mahfouz's *Midaq Alley* became the inspiration for my own personal conquest, which has guided me on an amazing journey through the past and present of Cairo. "Many things combine to show that Midaq Alley is one of the gems of times gone by and that it once shone forth like a flashing star in the history of Cairo. Which Cairo do I mean? That of the Fatimids, the Mamlukes, or the Sultans?"

Naguib Mahfouz's characters pass the same monuments and walk the same old history-drenched streets within the time frame of his novels and short stories as did the families and retainers of the Fatimid caliphs, the Mamluke princes, and the Ottoman sultans in the past.

After consulting with Mr. Mahfouz, I set out to visually translate his novels. Each photograph is based solely on the writing of Naguib Mahfouz. His locale is al-Gamaliya, the center of the original Fatimid city of al-Qahira, built in 973. Only his visual images were of interest to me, and so I dealt with self-imposed and self-explanatory boundaries.

My work is based on a search for beauty and pleasure that has been influenced and inspired by Mahfouz's writing. I aim to fulfill my desire to turn real life into a dream, which enables me to see the world as a beautiful illusion, and the real images achieve a new dignity. My photographs, spiritual and secular, are usually devoid of contemporary imagery in order to emphasize the work of Naguib Mahfouz.

His novel *The Journey of Ibn Fattouma* has a passage which exactly mirrors my feelings:

However much the place distances itself from me it will continue to let fall drops of affection, conferring memories that are never forgotten, and etching its mark, in the name of the homeland, in the very core of the heart. So long as I live I shall passionately love the effusions of the perfume vendors; the minarets and the domes; the radiant face of a pretty girl illuminating the lane; the mules of the privileged and the feet of the barefooted; the songs of the deranged and the melodies of the rebab; the prancing steeds and the lablab trees; the cooing of pigeons and the plaintive call of doves.

Mahfouz's Own Old Cairo

GAMAL AL-GHITANI

THE 80TH BIRTHDAY OF NAGUIB MAHFOUZ was marked by the Cairo University Center for Political Research and Study with a two-day symposium on the sociopolitical implications of his fiction. Novelist Gamal al-Ghitani, like Mahfouz, has made Old Cairo central to much of his fiction. Here he explores the city as manifested in Mahfouz's most ambitious work, the *Cairo Trilogy* of *Palace Walk*, *Palace of Desire*, and *Sugar Street:*

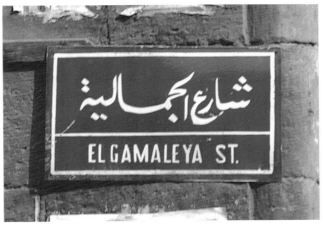

Old Cairo, the quarter of the city with which Mahfouz is most closely associated, remained for centuries the core of Egypt's capital. It was in this quarter that Mahfouz was born, in Bayt al-Qadi Square, at the heart of the area that provides the location for his most ambitious novel sequence, the *Cairo Trilogy.* The old city also forms the backdrop to many of Mahfouz's short stories, and to the novels *Khan al-Khalili* and *Midaq Alley.* The geography of the area might be read as a map of the novelist's imagination, setting perimeters to his fiction. Yet it is an area where Mahfouz lived for just twelve years. By the time Mahfouz was thirteen his parents moved to the then fashionable district of al-Abbasiya.

Old Cairo is an area that has remained almost intact. Buildings have deteriorated, shops and cafés have come and gone, but the major topographical features remain, and it is an area that has been spared the massive development that has affected the majority of Cairo's other quarters. It is still possible to take the steps taken by the characters in Mahfouz's novels. Many of the streets and alleys frequented by these characters retain the name Mahfouz used.

How successfully does Mahfouz depict old Cairo? It would of course be foolish to assume that the intention of the novelist—especially a novelist like Mahfouz—is simply to reproduce the features of a given place. Mahfouz neither aims to create documentaries nor attempts to write geography. Yet it remains an interesting exercise to explore the coincidences between imagination and reality as manifested in Mahfouz's novels, particularly the *Trilogy*.

Let me first look at *Palace Walk.* In this, the first part of the *Trilogy,* we are introduced to the area, in which all action takes place through the eyes of Amina. She stands at the window of her house, waiting for the return of her husband.

The novel opens with the precise description of the scene she observes. The street with its mosques, tombs, and drinking fountains, its shops and cafés, is described with such accuracy that it is, even now, perfectly possible to identify the site where most of the events in the novel take place.

The mashrabiya looks out to the Sabil of Bayn al-Qasrayn (Palace Walk) in al-Nahhasin (Coppersmith)

Street, which is lined with stores. If we walk this road from north to south we find the following Islamic monuments: Barquq Mosque, al-Nasir Muhammad Mosque, Qalawun Mosque, the Qalawun Baths, and the Qalawun Hospital.

On the other side of the street we see: Bashtak Palace, the Sabil of Bayn al-Qasrayn, the street that leads to Bayt al-Qadi Square, the Mausoleum and Madrasa of Saleh Nagm al-Din Ayyub, and al-Nahhasin Street.

Yet the area that is supposedly occupied by the home of Amina and her husband Ahmad Abd al-Jawad contains no domestic houses. The nearest residential districts are al-Khurunfish to the north and Harat al-Salihiya to the south. And the site described as being opposite the Sabil of Bayn al-Qasrayn (a public drinking fountain that does exist) is in reality occupied by a mosque. If Amina could see the minaret of Barquq from her window, then the house would have to be on the opposite side of the street. But if the location of the house is correct, she would not be able to see the Sabil of Bayn al-Qasrayn, which is across from Barquq, beside the Bashtak Palace.

In identifying actual locations we meet the same problem with Abd al-Jawad's shop. In chapter seven Mahfouz tells us that the shop lies in front of Barquq Mosque. Yet the site of the imaginary shop is occupied by a drinking fountain, the nearest shop being about 300

meters further south on al-Nahhasin Street. Mahfouz describes the location of the Ali Café, except there has not been a café here for a hundred years. And should we decide to sit in this café, we would not be able to see al-Ghuri from Harat al-Sanadiqiya, because the distance is too great.

In chapter twenty-one Mahfouz describes Umm Maryam's house as looking out onto Hammam al-Sultan, but in real-

ity this is the location of the Mausoleum and Madrasa of Saleh Ayyub. When Amina takes the fateful walk with Kamal to the mosque of Sayyidna al-Husayn, though, the description is absolutely correct.

The story of the first volume of the *Trilogy* ends in April of 1919, and the second volume, *Palace of Desire* (Qasr al-Shawq), starts six years later. Kamal is eighteen when he goes with his friend Fuad to Ahmad Abdu's café. This café existed in the 1930s, but was then replaced by Princess Shawikar's residence.

Perhaps we would be less interested in such anomalies in the geography of the novels if it were not for the fact that so much of what Mahfouz describes still exists. And his descriptions are concentrated within the very small area of al-Gamaliya. At no point in the seventy-one chapters of *Palace Walk* does a character travel more than three kilometers away. Even when Abd al-Jawad travels to Port Said, it is only his departure and return that are featured in the novel.

In *Palace of Desire* the topographical scope, at least, has grown. And the third novel of the trilogy, *Sugar Street* (al-Sukkariya), which deals with the decade following 1935, further expands the physical range of the earlier two novels.

Mahfouz consciously mixes the real places with streets that exist solely in his imagination. The city then becomes a cobweb of the real and the imagined. It is an imaginative landscape, constructed of elements so real that we occasionally confuse them with the city itself. Mahfouz gives himself the freedom to merge the real and imagined, which converge in a city that comes eventually to serve as a representation of his character's lives. Therein lies one of the fascinations of Mahfouz's *Trilogy.* In meshing the factual and verifiable with the imagination, Mahfouz loads his imaginary city with significances that echo down real streets and alleyways.

From "Naguib Mahfouz Remembers"

GAMAL AL-GHITANY

The Place

I have never come across anyone more attached to his place of birth than Naguib Mahfouz. He lived in the Gamaliya Quarter for the first twelve years of his life and then moved to the Abbasiya Quarter, but he has always remained attached to the people he came to know and who came to know him. This place has become the setting for his most important and greatest works.

During the summer, Naguib Mahfouz stops writing until the beginning of autumn, primarily because his eyes are subject to allergies in the summer air. On the first week of vacation, he goes to al-Husayn and to al-Gamaliya, and I often accompany him there and observe his various reactions. We walk through the streets and alleys where I myself grew up and lived for thirty years.

We started in Maydan al-Husayn and stopped in the center of it for a few moments. Naguib Mahfouz looked serene and confident; he appeared resigned to the surge of memories. He looked at the Azhar administration building. "The Khalil Agha Secondary School used to be here," he mused.

"In recent years the landmarks of the square have changed a number of times," I observed, "since some governor issued an order to demolish the famous Fishawi Café as well as a series of old buildings close to it."

"There used to be a clock standing in the middle of the square, and then they built a fountain, which was renovated and then surrounded by a small garden. About thirty years ago this same place used to serve as a terminal for the horse-drawn carriages bound for al-Darb al-Ahmar and al-Husayniya." Pointing to the *waqf* buildings to the west of the mosque, he said, "There used to be a green door here, a huge vault leading to a narrow alley that was the headquarters of the dervishes, the *majadhib* of the Husayn. You could see them sitting on both sides of the aisles."

I also recalled Maréchal 'Ali, the lunatic who wore a military uniform with many old decorations and Pepsi-Cola bottle caps, and the way he would carry a stick to shoo people away with. Naguib Mahfouz laughed out loud as he reminisced.

From Maydan al-Husayn we proceeded to a spot that served as an inspiration for one of his greater novels, *Zuqaq al-Midaqq (Midaq Alley)*. To reach Midaq Alley from the side of al-Azhar, we first had to go through Sanadiqiya Street, which was covered with dirt and the refuse of the stores and houses. Naguib Mahfouz noted regretfully, "These streets and alleys used to be swept clean twice a day: they used to sprinkle them with water. I personally remember the famous mule belonging to the municipality, the garage for carts, the stable of mules that was next to the judge's home." Mahfouz pointed out some buildings erected in the 1930s and recalled old homes surrounded by gardens that streched out to Midaq Alley. The alley is very narrow, no wider then five meters, and no longer then twelve. The coffeehouse was closed, because it was Sunday. There where three shops on the other side. "I remember that there was only the coffeehouse in the alley," he added. "I don't remember that house." In the middle of the alley stood a spice shop. Three elderly men sat in front of it.

"Is there still a bakery inside?" Mahfouz asked them.

"Yes. It seems you still remember the old times," the oldest answered. Mahfouz climbed the steps leading to the bakery, new steps now, built on the dirt road he had described in his novel. He looked at the bakery where Za'ita, the "maker of deformities," used to live.

"This is Naguib Mahfouz, the great writer," I whispered in the ear of one of the three old men.

After some hesitation he replied, "Is he the one who portrayed our alley in the movies?" I nodded yes. *"Ahlan wa sahlan!* Welcome!" he burst out, then lapsed again into his silence. We left the alley and the coffeehouse where Naguib Mahfouz used to mingle with his friends in bygone days.

So the idea behind Midaq Alley was born in this very spot—taking shape scene by scene, event by event—giving this narrow, forgotten place notoriety and fame. I recall one day when I accompanied an orientalist who insisted on seeing Midaq Alley. He came to the place, stood there contemplating it, and said laughing, "If Naguib Mahfouz wrote that extraordinary novel about this narrow, confined place, can you imagine what he could have accomplished if he had written about a thoroughfare like Shari' al-Azhar?"

The Souks

We proceeded to al-Hamzawi Souk, where the small shops of spices and perfumes still stand—where the souk still occupies the same spot it used to. It was a typical nineteenth-century Egyptian marketplace, without a counter between buyer and seller. Had this market existed in any European country, someone would have intervened to renovate it and turn it into a tourist attraction. From there we headed to the Gold Market. Mahfouz stopped at the entrance of the Salihiya Alley. Overhead stood the minaret of al-Salih Najm al-Din Ayyub, one of Cairo's oldest minarets, distinguished by its *mabkhara,* or "incenseburner," shape. It is considered a particularly early minaret design, from the period when the forms where first taking shape.

Naguib Mahfouz lingered for a few moments in front of a closed door and asked, "Is this still a coffeehouse?"

A passerby volunteered, "Yes, but today is Sunday."

"You know," he said, "this is the strangest coffeehouse—a long narrow alley with chairs on each side placed so that the customers almost touch the ones facing them. Things were different in our day."

We turned to the street of Mu'izz li-Din Allah. He pointed in the direction of an old house almost in ruins. "Some beautiful young women used to live in this house, and some of the rich and prominent men used to sit here, and just lift their eyes up to them and wink, twisting their proud moustaches. These were the accepted norms for flirtation and courtship in the 1920s and 1930s," he said, chuckling.

We moved through the copper market (Suq al-Nahhasin), where Mahfouz conceived of the place for Ahmad 'Abd al-Jawad's shop in *The Trilogy.* I noticed that he stared at some length into some corners while he walked slowly by others. In most instances he would lift his head as if meditating. At this point, I did not wish to disturb his memories with too many questions.

We walked past the historical monuments of Qalawun, the hospital, the bathhouse, the mosque, the dome of the mosque of al-Nasir Qalawun, and the mosque of Barquq. The minarets, especially those of Qalawun and Barquq, towered over the souks.

I turned to Naguib Mahfouz and said, "You have described this place where the house of Ahmad 'Abd al-Jawad stood in *The Trilogy*. If we go strictly by your description, there is no house standing here, but rather the mansion of the Prince Bashtak." Mahfouz agreed. We walked past the sultan's famous bathhouse, and he wondered, "Is it still standing?"

"Indeed it is," I replied, "and still in working order." I added that most of the Gamaliya bathhouses are still in working order. We reached the 'Abd al-Rahman Katkhuda public fountain and stopped for a few moments while Mahfouz pointed to the alley of al-Timbakshiya.

"This side used to be a souk exclusively for Syrian merchants. They used to sit in front of their stores, wearing huge yellow turbans, smoking their water pipes and displaying their merchandise: apricot paste, almonds, nuts, pistachios, and walnuts." He pointed to the remains of an old and spacious building. "This," he said, "used to be the mansion of the Muhaylimis, an important family. Some of them took part in the July 23rd revolution."

"Let's head toward the Bayt al-Qadi Square," I suggested. "We can pass by either the vaulted passage of Qirmiz or Bayt al-Qadi Alley."

"I was there a week ago," he said.

I added, "Then let's go to the other vaulted passage"

The Qur'an School (al-kuttab)

We started in the Bayt al-Qadi Quarter. "We used to call it al-Kababji Alley," he remarked. We walked past the historic tunneled passage where the family of Ahmad 'Abd al-Jawad had taken refuge during a World War II air raid, after which the hero of *The Trilogy* died. As the alley began to curve, Mahfouz pointed out some tall buildings. He said that they had not changed. He picked up his pace and went ahead of me toward the bend, where a historic fountain stood. I caught up with him, noticing that he appeared revitalized. "This is the *kuttab* (Qu'ran school) where I studied," he said. "The fountain still stands, but unfortunately the kuttab has been destroyed. It was on the upper floor, number nine." He pointed to the dilapidated upper floor, looked through the door, and turned to say that the stairs were still standing, though they were leading nowhere. At this point an old man approached him, asking, "Where are you from? Who are you looking for?"

I just said, "We are visitors."

We left Bayt al-Qadi, where Mahfouz was born at house number eight. We walked past Khan Ja'far Primary School and the Egyptian Club Hotel, where Mahfouz saw the very first moving pictures in Egypt. Then we came to the street of Mashhad al-Husayni where al-Husayn Mosque faces the historic fountain of Uthman, and right above it sits Bayn al-Qasrayn Primary School. "I studied here for several years," he said. He stared at the front of the school for a long while, and then we proceeded to the old Fishawi Café, which had been pulled down in 1969.

Not much remained of the original structure. When he was an employee at the Ghuri dome and the Waqf Ministry, Mahfouz used to spend long evenings and many hours here, smoking a water pipe and seeking inspiration for the heroes and events of his novels. "In those days," he noted sadly, unveiling his nostalgia, "the water pipes were enormous and tobacco came in many varieties and grades. Ya salam!" (Those were the days).

I had no idea what was going on in the mind of our great author, what far-off images were being conjured up. I only know that this place had marked him deeply, and that no other place had had such a great hold on his life as al-Gamaliya Quarter, al-Husayn, and this whole area, in spite of his residence in other parts of Cairo, in such quarters as al-'Abbasiya or al-Nil Street. He has never refelcted on those areas with the same intensity with which he portrayed al-Gamaliya, whose alleys remain the center of his world.

The Alley

In 1924, when Mahfouz was twelve years old, his family moved from the old house in Bayt al-Qadi to the house in 'Abbasiya (for which his father paid a thousand pounds). Naguib Mahfouz, however, remained drawn strongly to the Gamaliya Quarter, often visiting the Midaq Alley Coffeehouse, al-Fishawi, and one friend in particular who was a merchant in the Ghuriya Quarter. Mahfouz got married in the mid-1950s, moved to al-Nil Street in the suburb of al-'Aguza, and lived in a small, first-floor apartment overlooking the Nile. But he never lost his connections in al-Gamaliya. His yearnings for old Cairo remained powerful and overwhelming, and this old world and these ancient alleys formed the core of his works. He succeeded in refracting its spirit forcefully and truthfully, immortalizing the area in his writings.

The Cairo

of Naguib Mahfouz

... the closed cage formed by the wooden latticework ...

PALACE WALK / 2
View from Bashtak Palace looking south toward al-Ashraf Barsbay

*There was nothing to attract the eye except the minarets
of the ancient seminaries of Qala'un and Barquq*

PALACE WALK / 2
Minaret of the Madrasa of Barquq

*... Muhammad Ajami, the couscous vendor by the façade
of the seminary of al-Salih Ayyub ...*

... overlooking Mutawalli Gate, the minarets that shot up into the sky nearby, ...

PALACE WALK / 290
Minarets of the Mosque of al-Mu'ayyad

The minarets and domes fly up over the evening glow into the sky.

PALACE OF DESIRE / 165
Minarets and domes of al-Azhar

The muezzins went up to the balconies of their minarets to give thanks ...

PALACE WALK / 478
Minaret of al-Husayn

The façade was topped by a parapet with merlons
like spear points bunched tightly together.

PALACE WALK / 168
Mosque and Minaret of al-Husayn

... Shaykh Ra'uf at al-Bab al-Akhdar ...

PALACE WALK / 240–41
Minaret base of Ayyubid period, Mosque of al-Husayn

Others appeared to her as complete wholes, lacking details,
like the minarets of the mosques of al-Husayn, al-Ghuri, and al-Azhar.

"I visited the shrines of al-Sayyida Zaynab and of al-Husayn"

Domes of the Mausoleum of al-Sayyida Zaynab

He proposed a walk along New Street to al-Ghuriya.

PALACE WALK / 170
Entrance to the Mosque of al-Ghuri

The period he had spent studying at the University of al-Azhar had ended in failure.

MIDAQ ALLEY / 8
Sun-dial over the entrance to al-Azhar Mosque

At the end of the alley there was a little mosque of a Sufi religious order ...

PALACE WALK / 200
Tomb of Shaykh Sinan

... at Fishawi's café ...

MIRRORS, "SAQR AL-MANUFI"

God only knew what coffeehouses and friends the future had in store for him.

Ahmad Abduh's coffeehouse was a treasure for the dreamer.

And then there is its café known as Kirsha's.

"... Now we'll play a game of dominoes."

Shayk Mutawalli Abd al-Samad stood there in a crude, tattered, colorless gown ...

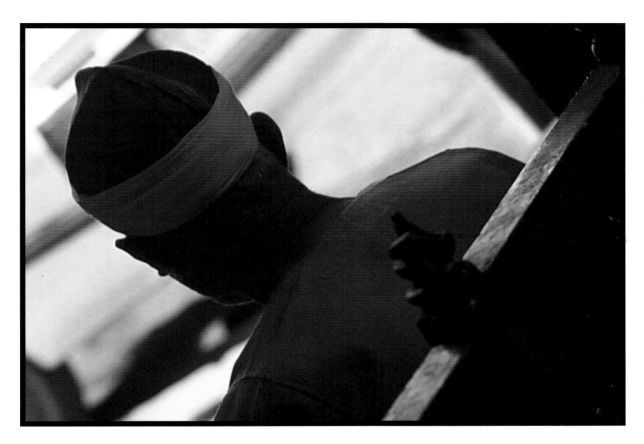

The venerable Sheikh Labeeb is an institution in our alley.

Outside every mosque there's a man who roams around with a censer,
wafting smoke over people for a pittance.

FOUNTAIN AND TOMB / 102

...a religious scholar from al-Azhar Mosque.

When his deliberate pace finally brought him to
the mosque of al-Husayn, he removed his shoes ...

SUGAR STREET / 131

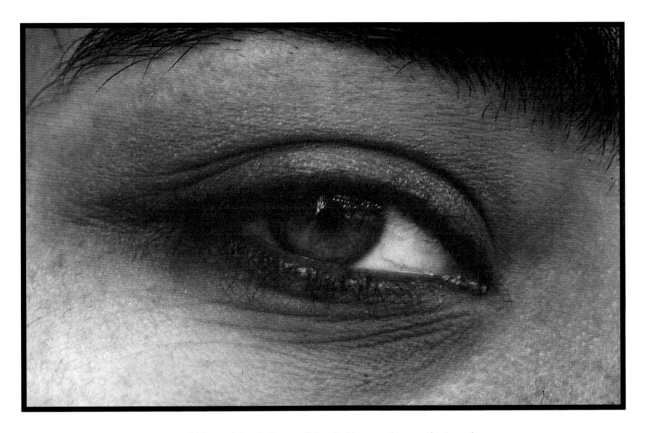

*... eyelids with delicate black lines along their edges
that enhanced her eyes and made them look splendidly clear.*

... a gypsy fortune-teller ...

PALACE WALK / 72

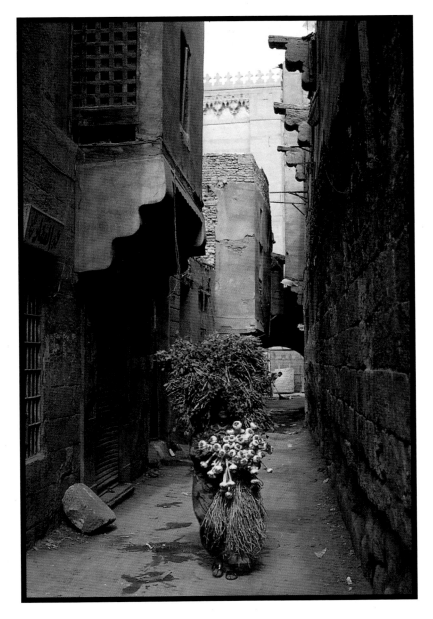

Her mother-in-law ruled the courtyard with the help of the maid Suwaydan.

PALACE WALK / 291

Near the Wikala-Sabil of Nafisa al-Bayda

... it was not the first time they had seen the sultana.

*"... Usually she'll be clean, with a refined appearance ...
She's often found at the vegetable market in al-Azhar Square."*

He taught us ... to smoke the goza, the buri, and the narghile ...

MIRRORS, "SAYYID SHOUAYR"

... retrieving the copper pots and pans that had been part of her trousseau.

Mr. Ya'qub was proposing to trade her the earrings for a bracelet.

Hanging from the ceiling was a large lantern ...

It would be a large, bound volume about the size and shape of the Holy Qur'an.

Hajj Darwish, who sold beans ...

... al-Bayumi, the drinks vendor...

... al-Fuli, the milkman ...

"Shaddad Bey Abd al-Hamid is the greatest of all the cotton merchants ..."

Mr. Ibrahim al-Far, the copper merchant ...

... al-Sayyid Ahmad Abd al-Jawad reached his store,
situated in front of the mosque of Barquq on al-Nahhasin Street ...

"... His place has been taken by a watchmaker ..."

They were shopping for various types of perfume
useful in promoting delight and beauty.

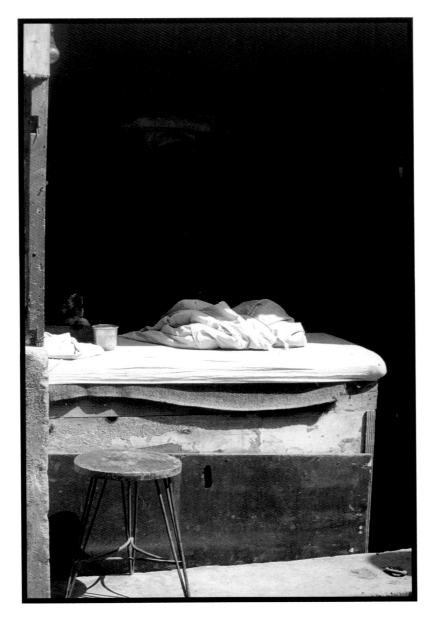

... as an apprentice at an ironing shop in Khan Ja'far ...

... a coal merchant in the Mubayyada region of al-Gamaliya.

... the table on which the scales were placed ...

... one of our local young men works in the copper shop...

It had become a fez shop, where new ones were sold and old ones blocked.
The copper forms and the heating apparatus were up in front.

Its enclosed balcony looked down on al-Gamaliya Street ...

PALACE WALK / 78

The carriage proceeded along Palace Walk ...

... the window belonged to the residence of Zubayda the chanteuse.

At the end he could see Palace Walk
and the entrance of Hammam al-Sultan.

... the doorway of the ancient hospital of Qala'un.

PALACE WALK / 173

He approached Qirmiz Alley with its vaulted roof ...

PALACE WALK / 50
Madrasa of Mithqal over Qirmiz Alley

... he saw one side of Bab al-Futuh.

PALACE WALK / 445

*She stood there this morning with her eyes wandering from Hammam al-Sultan
to the ancient building that housed the public cistern.*

The Sabil-Kuttab of Katkhuda and Bashtak Palace

He was looking behind him at Bab-Mutawalli ...

PALACE WALK / 273
Dome of the Sabil of Tusun Pasha with the minarets of al-Muayyad Mosque

The landmarks of the ancient district hand down the wisdom of past generations.

Gate in Khan al-Khalili

The sight of Muhammad Iffat's house in al-Gamaliya was a familiar and beloved one for Ahmad Abd al-Jawad.

SUGAR STREET / 34
Bayt al-Sihaymi

... the courtyard garden was marvelous.

SUGAR STREET / 34
Bayt al-Sihaymi

They went on until they reached Khan Ja'far Primary School, ...

He decided to relax for a while. He stayed in a suspect hotel in the Muski ...

MIRRORS, "SAYYID SHOUAYR"

The car carried them swiftly to Bab El Nasr
and stopped at a place where the graves were built in the open.

"He's buried in the clothes he was wearing next to Sheikh Yunis' tomb."

Sources of the Extracts

Palace Walk. Trans. William M. Hutchins and Olive E. Kenny. Cairo: The American University in Cairo Press, 1989.

Palace of Desire. Trans. William Maynard Hutchins, Lorne M. Kenny, and Olive E. Kenny. Cairo: The American University in Cairo Press, 1991.

Sugar Street. Trans. William Maynard Hutchins and Angele Botros Samaan. Cairo: The American University in Cairo Press, 1992.

Midaq Alley. Trans. Trevor Le Gassick. Cairo: The American University in Cairo Press, 1985.

Fountain and Tomb. Trans. Soad Sobhy, Essam Fattouh, James Kenneson. Washington, D.C.: Three Continents Press, 1991.

The Harafish. Trans. Catherine Cobham. Cairo: The American University in Cairo Press, 1994.

Mirrors. Trans. Roger Allen. Cairo: The American University in Cairo Press, 1999.

The Beginning and the End. Trans. Ramses Awad. Ed. Mason Rossiter Smith. Cairo: The American University in Cairo Press, 1985.